SMOTE

SMOTE

POEMS

JAMES KIMBRELL

Sarabande Books
LOUISVILLE, KENTUCKY

FIRST EDITION

Library of Congress Cataloging-in-Publication Data

Kimbrell, James, 1967–
  [Poems. Selections]
  Smote : poems / James Kimbrell.—First edition.
     pages ; cm
  ISBN 978-1-941411-09-4 (softcover : acid-free paper)
  I. Title.
  PS3561.I41677A6 2015
  811'.54—dc23

                              2014047731

Cover and interior by Kirkby Gann Tittle.

Manufactured in Canada.

This book is printed on acid-free paper.

Sarabande Books is a nonprofit literary organization.

 The Kentucky Arts Council, the state arts agency, supports
Sarabande Books with state tax dollars and federal funding from the
National Endowment for the Arts.

for Jami

CONTENTS

ACKNOWLEDGMENTS

I would like to thank the editors and staff of the following publications in which several of the poems in this collection first appeared.

The Cincinnati Review: "How to Tie a Knot," "Pluto's Gate: Mississippi," "There's Nothing Wrong with You"

Connotation Press: "Take Me As I Am"

Narrative: "Ode: Feeling Up My Friend's Sister at the Moment Their Drunken Father Begins the Dog Slaughter"

The New Guard: "Love Letter to You, Dear Reader"

New South: "O Anna Lynn, You Must Have Known," "It Was Like a Movie," "The Guitar Boat"

The Normal School: "So Many Stories"

Ploughshares: "Chicken Brick'n," "Free Checking!" "Smote"

Southern Poetry Review: "The Full Ratio," "Not Soul"

"How to Tie a Knot" also appeared in *Best American Poetry 2012*, edited by Mark Doty.

"How to Tie a Knot" and "Smote" also appeared on *Poetry Daily*.

My sincere gratitude to Florida State University for their support during the period in which these poems were written. Also, my thanks to John and Renée Grisham and the University of Mississippi for a fellowship that afforded me a nine-month residency in which much of this work was begun. Lastly, my eternal gratitude for the continued encouragement and editorial acumen of Adam Boles, Erin Belieu, Robert Olen Butler, John Deming, Kerry James Evans, Juan Carlos Galeano, Chris Hayes, Robert Herschbach, Judy Jordan, Jami Kimbrell, Chris Mink, C. Leigh McInnis, and Jane Springer.

SMOTE

"... then we shall know that it is not his
hand that smote us: it was chance."

I Samuel 6:9

1

Free Checking!

Desire for the good deal, the hot need
to look slick, wordless advertisement
for the invisible product, I release you
like the dumpster behind the cafeteria

releases these long, festering rivers of milk.
Fear of death, fear of narrow spaces, love
of the wine-red mole that punctuates
the transaction-inspiring cleavage of Jill,

my credit union teller, I release you like
the scared shitless man releases the tiny
parachute. The name "James Kimbrell"
which I share (says Jill) with thirty-eight people

in Florida alone, the subsequent deflation
of our hero groomed by the goddess,
sped by the wind, loved by his mutt, envy
of his entire dreamed-up Mediterranean—

I release you like the crank-addled truck driver
releases his cargo at the midnight dock
until the warehouse is one in a trail
of crumbs, little light left on behind him.

So Many Stories

—for April

To return to the living, you have to walk backward
from that place where every beer joint has a playground
and no one's afraid of happiness guaranteed to end.

Why am I here? Why did my sister disappear? Waves
of foam washing up around her comatose mouth,
helicopter worthy. Soothsayer of katydids, reader

of bees inside the pink hibiscus, who am I asking?
In the land of her absence, everyone is allotted
so many tears. To return to the living, you need

to notice the dogs at our feet, anxious for scraps,
dust rolling in from the funeral next door. Why
did my sister get tossed by her belt loop out the back

of some cinder-block excuse for a bar? Why death
beside a utility pole? Tiller of clouds, augur of
whatever, when the answer arrives, do us a favor.

How to Tie a Knot

If I eat a diet of rain and nuts, walk to the P.O.
in a loincloth, file for divorce from the world of matter,
say *not-it!* to the sea oats, *not-it!* to the sky
above the disheveled palms, *not-it!* to the white or green oyster boats
and the men on the bridge with their fishing rods
that resemble so many giant whiskers,
if I repeat *this is not it, this is not why I'm waiting here,*
will I fill the universe with all that is not-it
and allow myself to grow very still in the center of
this fishing town in winter? Will I look out past the cat
sleeping in the windowsill and say *not-it!* garbage can,
not-it! Long's Video Store, until I happen upon what
is not *not-it?* Will I wake up and *BEHOLD!*
the "actual," the "real," the "awe-thentic," the *IS?*
        Instead I walk down to the Island Quicky, take a pound
of bait shrimp in an ice-filled baggie, then walk to the beach
to catch my dinner. Now waiting is the work
I'm waiting for. Now the sand crane dive-bombs the surf
of his own enlightenment because everything
is bait and lust and hard-up for supper.
        I came out here to pare things down,
wanted to be wind, simple as sand, to hear each note
in the infinite orchestra of waves fizzling out
beneath the rotting dock at five o'clock in the afternoon
when the voice that I call *I* is a one-man boat
slapping toward the shore of a waning illusion.
Hello, waves of salty and epiphanic distance. Good day,
bird who will eventually
go blind from slamming headfirst into the water.
What do you say fat flounder out there
deep in your need, looking like sand speckled with shells,

lying so still you're hardly there, lungs lifting
with such small air, flesh both succulent and flakey
when baked with white wine, lemon and salt, your eyes
rolling toward their one want when the line jerks, and the reel
clicks, and the rod bends, and you give up
the ocean floor for a mouthful of land.

Pluto's Gate: Mississippi

—for Private First Class C. Leigh McInnis

I appear to be a full-on rich guy
wheeling into Oxford
down the cedar-lined drive across from William Faulkner's
determined to shield myself (my fancy wristwatch
                      my roadster
                      both used both fast as hell) from the shame
I once knew in this my state
beneath my bowl-cut
my underwear of the dead
my hand-me-down teeth
and at the first supper club I light upon—three gins in—I say to this
    woman
Khayat is of Lebanese descent
        No hell! no he ain't she says
           nearly hysterical in her insistence that *no prez of ole mizz*
                              could be a sandnigger
I ask her where do you go to church
                          Saint Johns she says
tell Father Hadeed I said hi
tell him I said Alhamdulilla
tell him the ghost of Bill Faulkner quoth to me
                            quail fly south in the afternoon
                            better pray often
                            better pray soon
for those students in '64 crossing Lynch Street
                  on the way to Jackson State
                  white drivers speeding up
                  dubbed it "blacktopping"
how much shit can one people take
consider the white family walking down Ellis
carrying their groceries

                        too poor for even the most worn out hooptie
the youngest amongst them a little boy
                        —*Hey y'all!*—
totes among other items
a sweaty gallon of milk
that has burst a jagged seam in the paper sack
                              so that he cradles the whole mess
                              with both arms as if carrying a sick baby
                              and that was rough but
no one swerved to hit us
Jesus of the Confounderacy
Jesus of the Union
because I love my schoolmates
that never left
                  black white Pakistani
                  Choctaw Lebanese quadroons
women with hair piled to dangerous heights
that saved me from my youth
I love kibbeh and the swamp
I love the heat
                  O hellish dome as soon as I could
I packed my junk and was gone
                              gone in my ragged out Plymouth Belvedere
with its push button transmission
and sawed-off seatbelts
my face stinging like a stuck voodoo doll
red with the turpentine curse of that place
I especially did not love
                  on that particular day the Sergeant Major in the meeting
                  of non-commissioned officers
                  scheduling guard drills around MLK's birthday

12

says shoot six more
we'll take the whole week off
        —oooh this sure is a tell-all!—
well yes though I don't dare tell C. Leigh
after drill when we're heading to his place
in the old neighorhood
where we'll eat a free bucket of chicken because Monica still works at
    Popeye's
and we're going to watch Prince videos
and not drink beers
because for whatever reason we're both sober
and on our way
everyone stares us down
like the only time they saw a black and a white guy
in a car together was when
they were cops
and I tell C. Leigh a dream I have betimes
                    I'm back at our old house on Hooker Street
                  always a black family surprised to see whitey
                          and I'm so white in this dream
                          you can barely see me
                          white as a polar bear's pillow case
                          white as the ear fuzz
                          of the great Johnny Winter
but they see me and I see them seeing me
I say back then my bed was behind the table
here's the notch I cut with a steak knife
when I was three
               and for the first time—eyes wide—they believe me
the little girl her hand on her hip
says *let me guess whitebread*

grew up poor

        wants to do some good

                just what we need

                        Starbucks!

I say we were so poor I still get nervous in Starbucks
boo fricking hoo she says *you still white*
white as Gods white-ass golf balls
I say shoot me already
                at which point her mother brings the gun
when she pulls the trigger the confederate flag pops out
the mother says *just kidding you want some dinner*
and this time when she shoots
the table is covered
with turnips cornbread little cups
of mayonnaise colored pudding
what you looking at she says *better eat your dinner*
and the three of us say an honest grace
grateful uneasy
            Lord we say
            we need wings to match the other wings
            we don't have
            we need a bubbling we can hold
            Yahweh Hot Rod Sky Talker
            talk to us Mister Master
            Cloud Cork of the Transcendent Cava
            Amen and Amen
but when we open our eyes
the food has vamoosed
and we all cry out stumbling in that wilderness
if we had soup we could have soup and crackers
if we had crackers . . . but of course

we don't because love comes on like a weight
and a claw and a sucker-punch
and in the case of Mississippi
gateway to this our under-country
history is the dish that leaves us skinny
petrified forest of narcotic tornadoes
Scratch's bullwhip
devil's dancefloor
crackhead's cruise ship
backwoods Medusa with a kudzu afro
whose green gaze
sprouts branches from the fluted
columns of Beauvoir
   O hold my hand brother
before we return
peckers in the dirt of our poke salad geography
redeemed as empty Faygo bottles
in the burned down shed
in the bamboo patch
behind Bilbo's poolhall

Take Me As I Am

—after Basic Training

Let me take the Trailways far from the barracks of Bravo Company
to my father's corner of the ramshackle fourplex
with its stairwell that smells like motor oil and beer,
Aqua Velva, cigars and critter piss, like the armpit
of dilapidated Jackson itself, and when I arrive to no
running water, let me shuck my Class A's and walk
beside my father with a bar of soap. In our cut-offs
and flip-flops, let us stroll with a total absence of stealth
up the hill to the Bel Aire with its lovely unguarded swimming pool
where we'll set our beers down by the lawn chairs
and swim a lap for appearances' sake, big orange August moon
hanging over the rooftops like a busted bicycle reflector.
Let me stay there for a sudsy moment with my old man—
miles from marching, let me forget how to lock and load
my twenty round clip and shoot the green pop-up targets
shaped like humans with no arms. And when people
who actually live in the Bel Aire walk by the pool and we wave
to them, let them say hi like they would to any swimmers
because we do look like rent-paying neighbors
in the second before they register the underwater light
like a train's beam shining through the shallow end,
and the two men, the son and his father, up
to their chests in a widening nest of soap bubbles.

Ode: Feeling Up My Friend's Sister at the Moment Their Drunken Father Begins the Dog Slaughter

It's like instant punishment for the nipple she shows me, the pinkish tender at my fingertips before her father pumps the first shells into the chamber, before the original buckshot blast, the initial yelp, the first half-dead dog twitching in the grass.

•

The wire-haired terrier is the last, little blur of salt and pepper, the smallest target, though I suspect she must have once been the family favorite, the not-yet-picked-off, so fast, so sweet that their father, in a kinder moment, named her after his favorite rolling paper: *Zig Zag*.

•

O heart above his biker's belly, steady pumper, what whiskey, what blow, what fuel in her father who I imagine, by now, shooting himself in the mouth, his head flying apart, then re-assembling for a homicidal eternity in some dogless ring of hell.

•

She takes her shirt at the waist and pulls it up slowly: first her hips, then her belly. Then her bra—yellow button-sized flowers on the white shoulder straps. And when she places my hand on her breast, my fingertips run rough and nicked

•

across the smooth fabric. I can't speak. I can hardly breathe. I consider myself lucky, a knock-kneed idiot in a crooked barn gone to heaven:

her shoulders, her hair, and then, uncupped, her untanned breasts in the dust-funneled air.

·

Their dogs are healthy, their dogs are kind, do not bite. Their dogs heel cattle, run off from time to time, but not after log trucks, and never too far. Their dogs are puppies. Their dogs are old. Their dogs are all shoveled into a single hole.

·

Minus Zig Zag: down from the hayloft, then off with her brother on his Honda 70 to the front yard where Zig Zag is running in a tightening circle while their father reloads, and we speed out, and I swoop Zig Zag up, yes, into my arms.

·

Who would guess that the father would take another shot despite the fact of me and his son between the barrel and the dog? We hear buckshot whiz by, and do not, thank God, bog down in mud between the edge of their yard and the highway.

·

To say that this was punishment would force reason. I touched her breasts, felt her nipples. Then the first shot. I don't know what it's about, which is what I tell my neighbor decades later after she walks out from putting her son to bed,

•

sweet boy who was pulled from her womb past the cord around his neck, beautiful boy who has only learned slowly, carefully, how to speak with damaged muscles, who says to her in the moment before sleep: "Mom, I'm afraid. What if I can never sing?"

The Starting Point

1.

It was good to be a finalist in the Future Farmers of America
extemporaneous speech contest. It was bad to snort
what we called "Rush" (isobutyl nitrite?) with my buddies
before taking the podium so that I floated up

> and hovered a good ten feet above my body,
> the whole auditorium turning dog-dick pink
> as I yammered on about leadership and agribusiness.

2.

It's not so wide, that corn row with its this-side-living, this-side-not.

3.

I wasn't allowed to march with the band.
Apparently, you can't just fake it.

After a month in the HVAC basement,
I mastered the first nine notes to the theme song of "Dallas."

What does it mean to ask, are the dead
proud of us?

As it was in that underworld, as it is in every other.

What comes first, the moron or the mirror?

J. R. Ewing, get up, we love you!

Every few days the band director would clomp down the stairs,
glower at my saxophone,
hard-sell the tuba.

We call it *under* because it's in the past,
not some cave-mouth above hell.

2

Apology after Driving Down Hooker Street Thirty
Years after We Moved

Cottrell, I come to you all grown up and ignorant
of your current address. I come like a name
on a bucktoothed billboard, like absence
in a mirror, like daylight in a sock
                              when saying ran sideways—

        —that your sister, his daughter, was *half* of anything,

to say *anything* meant assaulting a silence
silently agreed upon, yes, but even then we both knew
you don't insult money,
                          which is printed on cotton and the tongue
that speaketh ambition,
                —recurring dream of breaking fucking loose—

which itself is like a railroad yard
where one car humps another, banging bones
like a collision of pissed-off dinosaurs
echoing through the soon to be re-possessed air

                        where we shoot hoops
                        in the dark through a spokeless bicycle rim
                        bolted to plywood,
                        nailed to an oak.

                        •

Hooker Street hookers! Hooker Street hookers! How sweetly sang
the neighborhood kids on our bored
trudge from school.

It was wise to slug each other, if only to distract them.

Cottrell, I'm sorry I pulled loose a patch of your fro, that you jerked free
a fistful of my feathered do, carefully combed.
Sorry, too, that when we stood up
from the stalemate dirt,

> I opened my hand—
> a few of your hairs
> took wind—a few stuck
> to my palm like
> black dandelion fronds in a sheen of Sta-Sof.

·

I think of the white man with five white strands
combed over to resemble at least ten.
Everybody pays their style dues, Cottrell,
even your sister's father.

> It's not my place to apologize, but I do.

I can't say if your mother loved that man.
Maybe she despised him showing up
each Wednesday in his dingy blue Benz,

> edging up to the curb
> like some double-life
> archetype of white Jackson
> fearful of being seen.

He walked in the front door—you bolted out the back,
slammed the basketball into the dirt
until I looked out from the house across the street
then came on over because sweat, dust, and leather
make for some caked-up hands
and pretty good friends,
though, as I was want to point out,
you weren't much of challenge for me, one-on-one,
you trash-talking sucker.
                            And then in the middle of another instance
of clearly letting you defeat me,
the diesel sedan
cranks like an expensive tractor, chortles off toward Eastover,

                            and I head across the street beneath the deafening moon
when your mother appears in her nightgown at the kitchen window,
though she never seems to see me.
Maybe it was the inside light.
Maybe the unlit night
I passed through when she unlatched the screen door
because no one said a word,
                    because the man was gone,
                    and she could allow
                    her own son
                    back inside the house.

It Was Like a Movie

in which we moved to Leakesville, little town whose name
conjured images of a urinal or a mile-wide ceiling drip.
Town that, minus one vowel, would have been "LAKES-ville,"
which is how everyone pronounced it anyway. It was like
a movie that got turned around and in which our hero
suffers from dementia: he stares into the camera of eternity
and lip syncs *Hi Mom! Hi Mom!* for the remainder of his
demented, motherless days. But in the beginning it was
still the two of us, me and Mom, having just moved
into a clapboard house with cinder blocks for porch steps
and where, not two months before, an old woman died
in the bed that she slept in for years, bed that became mine
so that I could feel this old woman's shape like a drained
pond in the mattress beneath me. It was like a movie of a house
in which lived only a woman and her son, and behind
which stretched a blighted pecan orchard; behind that,
the Magnolia Cemetery, its little maze of oystershell roads
in slow dissolve as the young divorcée walked to work
on that first morning down the hill to the nursing home,
her son sleeping in the house behind her, house in which
there was not much food. When I woke I heard the voices
of children across the street, bouquet of scrambled eggs
and bacon guiding me forward. That morning, I heard
a ghost ahead of me, matching my steps. I was not the ghost
that morning, but the one who heard the ghost,
smelled food through the open window, then walked
across the street where all the kids seemed so shocked
to see me it was as if they'd never met a stranger.
I walked past them and up to the screen door and said hello
to their mother, Ms. Anna, who slaved away
in the sweltering kitchen where flies stuck like raisins

to the yellow strip hanging above the sink. She never let me
wash a single dish, though she fed me each day that summer
when my mother vanished into her job
down the long moan-filled halls of the nursing home.
Ms. Anna, who loved me for no reason that I understood,
who taught me how to bathe kittens, how to always talk
sweetly to them, soothing away their panic in the wide
scrub bucket—that town, that time, became so much
like a movie it began to disturb me. It only got worse.
I was playing with Charlie, Ms. Anna's youngest son,
exploring a distant corner of the Magnolia Cemetery
when I saw a picture embossed on a porcelain plaque
in the middle of a rose-tinted granite stone, picture of a boy
with short brown hair and glasses and late summer tan,
boy to whom I bore enough of a resemblance that I
couldn't help but keep looking. Charlie explained
that last summer, his oldest brother was moving a rifle
from the truck parked in their backyard: the rifle
went off, shot toward one brother's ear, took a chunk
of his ear lobe, then passed clear through the throat
of the neighbor boy whose grave this was. He said the boy
died instantly, little dome of blood mixed with spit
bubbling up at the corner of his mouth.

It was true what
people said, that
I looked just like
this boy. That no
one can stop
that movie when
my mother
befriends a new man,

an even worse
drunk than my
father; she smokes
and smokes until,
ten years after
she quits, she dies
in a nursing home not
unlike the one where
she gave each patient
their daily ration
of cigarettes, nor when my
sister joins us
in Leakesville at the end
of that summer,
begins dating the boy
she will marry,
raises two kids,
and the week after
the youngest one
moves out, my sister
gets diagnosed—
cancer, stage four.
Movie in which my father
gets sober when I
am grown, moves
in with me in Florida
on the tail-end of
the century's worst hurricane
and in the same
week of my sister's
diagnosis, discovers

he too has a tumor
in his lung roughly
the size of a fortune cookie
so that everyone
is in a panic, and soon
I'm surrounded by
people I love and who
are no longer here (I
should not mention
my oldest sister who
that same month
drank herself into
a coma, or that my wife
drove south with
our infant daughter—statue
of a breadcrumb,
white bird in a white
field—I love you,
I miss you—as this
would push the limits of
what a movie
can hold) my
sister still fighting,
then vanished,
my father gone,
my mother equally
invisible, my days
spent sniffing
the sweat in the leather
hatband of my dad's
gray fedora, wondering

why I've been spared,
and what to do
with my father's wallet,
his Sam's Club card,
anxious to clean,
to toss out all but
the essentials, to save
my daughter from the future
work of ordering my life
after my life
because I will not
be surprised by death,
having already been
surprised by living,
my nights spent
rehearsing conversations
that took place
years ago, or saying
what I never said
to people now
impossible to speak to,
or rewinding what
of the past can be
rewound as if
to discover some clue.
One Sunday after church, Ms. Anna (who, by this time,
took me everywhere) carried me to the potluck.
An old man, his plate in his lap, asked if I'd gone
deer hunting, if my father had taken me fishing
that summer. I'd never met this man who clearly thought
he knew me. It was like a movie in which I made up

answers to this man's questions, not knowing how
not to. A movie in which the man realized that the boy
he believed I was had been dead for a year, shot
in an accident. The man stood up and walked away,
white-faced, shaken. A movie in which I was someone
who knew no one, whom everyone knew. A stranger
who was already one of them, larger than life,
stronger than death, a dead boy, a star, though there
were no theaters in Leakesville, and we owned no
television, no car, and so were residents of a world
in which, for all practical purposes, movies did not exist.

Smote

Even stones had a purpose in falling: they were going
home to Earth, their proper place.
—Rupert Sheldrake, *The Presence of the Past*

When Shirley Weems submarines her Barbie
in the shallows, spooking the catfish
while her brother and me sit on upturned buckets
with cane poles on our side of the pond
not bothering anybody, I note
how the light around Shirley seems so rosy,
all a'twinkle with its own
self-contained Shirley music. I pick a dirt clod
I don't think has a rock in it, but it hangs
long above the pond before completing
its arc, smacking Shirley
upside the head, which sets her off screaming
for the house where her grandfather—big
Truman Weems—barrels out
in these overalls it looks like he's stuffed full
of inflated innertubes, what you might call
stacked fat, like raw biscuits
pushing against the cardboard tube
after you whack the can against
the counter edge—so puffed out
and defined is Mr. Truman's fat that each roll
trundles separately when he charges
after me, slapping the air, hollering
that I'd better get back across the street,
and where is my mother, I am nothing
but trouble—*Little lousy*
knobhead son of a bitch!
                        Thank you, Mr. Truman,
for your patience and understanding.
In my defense, I threw the dirt clod

because I never thought it would reach her.
Because she was scaring off all the fish
no one would ever catch anyway.
I threw it because she was so pretty, or lonely, or I was.
I tried to lob it more or less around her,
and yet with that one mistake
I joined the ranks of the rock throwers,
and it shook me so biblically
I thought I'd dreamed it.
                    Even the Guernsey cows
grazing in the pecan orchard between
my house and the cemetery
seemed suspicious,
disappointed. Those sweet drowsy cows,
weed munchers, cows never milked,
old absent landlord cows, they stare
at me now with no more comprehension
or pardon than on that day
when I found
the very reach of the earth vaster, more
unforgiving than I ever
imagined in the tall grass littered with rotten pecans
where I lay at the feet
of the animals.

Apocalyptic Lullaby

Walking across the snow
to the garage behind my house
in Mt. Vernon, Ohio,
crooked and cold garage
where I'd tinker
with this old pawn-shop Stratocaster
deep in my post-divorce blues,
I did not expect
to open the door and find
a teenage couple going at it
like sheep in a prospect
of sun-dappled rye grass
between the mower and my erstwhile
weightlifting bench.
    It was sweet how he draped
his stomach, his whole
torso over her back as if to shield
her, or himself, from my view.
What could I do? I said pardon.
I closed the door quietly
and walked toward
the house and tried not
to look out the kitchen window
like the envious creep
I didn't want to become,
the one who, it occurs
to me now, might have been trying
to tell me something true, ever
applicable: there's always porn.
Always memory. Always
a good reason to live alone,

to stand outside the radius
of love and witness
the goings-on of shoulders,
breasts, the inimitable
glory and mess of romance
and hair and the brackish
scent that, an hour
later, lingered there.
The world will never end.

The Full Ratio

. . . the possession is Infinite & himself Infinite.
—William Blake, *There Is No Natural Religion*

Witness this woman's knees locked
in position half out of her parked car,
her fists clenched, her arms stuck
as if mid-jumping jack. She rocks
from the waist up, pitches close
to falling to the hot pavement dotted
with spit-out gum and bits of glass,
her stunned *I don't know, I don't*
know what's wrong with me
like something I hear through a seashell
then run toward.
                              I do what I'm told
by the dispatch operator. I hold
her head back and repeat each fact: she's
thirty-two, no heart attacks, not
diabetic, not in a wreck. She wears her black
hair pulled back and I have no
idea what—maybe dog days, the July
of everything—pinned her to this spot
in the grocery store parking lot
where she cannot unhinge
herself, her arms still skyward
as if reaching for a trapeze
that's swinging right toward her
even as they strap her
to the padded blue stretcher.
         I stand there recalling
the details as if they might
still matter: the ambushed look,
how her throat was sweating
though her forehead was ashen,

beaded white of deodorant
in the creases of her armpits,
a few televised-looking
onlookers. How could they know
that I've waited half my life
to wave with a hero's hand,
to hold without knowing it
and repeat without knowing it
everything's okay until the ambulance
pulls away, the buggies breeze
freely past, and the clouds
well up like hurt feelings above the pine-tops
where the usual seagulls
wheel high then low again, off-course,
confused because the pavement
with yellow and white lines
is not the ocean.

Roots

in the diesel of rotten potato flies
and sour milk leaking out the side
one man raised
a trash can
in the year before the mini-series
one man pulled the lever
worked the crusher's
commotion in the year
before Master and Kizzy
one man grabbed a lid
while another ran ahead
all of them hollering
back and forth

another self-portrait disguised
(worse crime) as grandiose
idealization of working-class
descendants of slaves
by he who makes a profession
of writing on the breezeway

when I pedaled
my bike down the gravel drive
and said *hi* one man
wiped his forehead
with the back of his glove
called me little man—
what's up little man
how you doing
little man

little man big poet in the diesel of
mid-June Jackson
you have no idea

you want your children to play
with garbage men
you want your grandchildren
to load roach-bait coffee grounds
rank ass egg shells
who's your hero now
bon hypocrite?

one man jumped up
and stood on the back bumper
his boots
high above pavement
the truck rounding
the corner giving him
the appearance of flight
or levitation one
man little man
waited most Wednesdays
for their arrival

and isn't that
your mother hazy
in the background
representing the moral
element—radiance
of folded towels balanced
in her slender arms—
saying garbage men
made next to nothing
by which you know
damn well what she meant

little man had the makings
of a fine communist

I was hoping for a system
of barter everyone
performs a service receives
all in turn—each
necessary task equal
in its necessity

why not just say one black man
or do you mean to imply
that all garbage men are black
and so naturally everyone
would understand that
another testament to your little
man mind over-baked
in the scrappy shade
of your cherished yet wholly
inadequate magnolia

little man saw the movie *Roots*
in third grade too
his friends circled him screamed
we're not your slave anymore
screamed "honkey honkey"
to which he replied "nigger
nigger" until all voices
finally wore out and no one really apologized
I don't know if we had a word yet
for that kind of sorry
but the day grew longer
than our collective history
and we all went back
to pitching pennies
against the brick wall
behind the lunchroom

write this, little man: one man
Medgar Evers stepped from his car
cradling t-shirts that read "Jim Crow
Must Go!" then one man
crouching issued his own soul
forth to eternity in white hell
his Enfield rifle
behind the camellias by the driveway
and the trash cans

one garbage man had a pic of Muhammad Ali
on his baseball cap
which little man remembers
in problems of philosophy
fly like Schopenhauer
sting like Nietzsche
and like at least
half the white people there
he wanted flies
on the grave of Byron De La Beckwith
—of the other half he recalled
from childhood despairingly
one Westside Baptist Church rule: don't wear your Cub Scout uniform to
    school
the blacks will see it
and want to join

at long last little man grows up
aimless joint that aimless college
who picks up your garbage now
what's his name what's his life like
how much acid did you drop
hey little man didn't I see you

at the Chi O swap
now keep that mess on your side
of the wide
lily white page

after my eight a.m. Mickey
Mouse math (still too
difficult for me) I lay
down in my dorm room
dreamed I was walking down the hall
on my way to nap
on my door was a thumbtacked dollar bill
on which someone left
a message or a poem
but when I tried to read it
it turned to bits
and floated around
like plastic snow in a plastic globe
so I walked in and there on my bed
I saw a newspaper
the headline read local boy
wins award
then that too flew into pieces
then re-assembled
on my closet door
into a black-and-white poster
of LeVar Burton
as Kunta Kinte he was holding
his hands up
his chains still on
but his shackles broken

his palms out
as if he'd been there
waiting for me
calling my name

My Father's Friends Travel from the Afterlife to Attend His Memorial

Cold pals of Kingfish, cock-eyed pool sharks, handlers
of mysterious auto parts, men who took a decade in jail
like a skinned knee, Uncles A–Z, you arrive in pairs
like beautiful old shoes no one will ever wear again.
You storage shed keepers of cash behind the case
of Nehi bottles, shades who appear, calling me, as before,
Little George—
                   I have let you all down. No firearms.
No town car. No here's a quarter call Johnny Zesso.
I traded that line for a gull, a song. I survey, gussied,
over-taut, starched shirt worthy of the funeral banquet,
and wonder what you would hock for one day
of my clarity.
                   O Hebrew singers of Greek, Arabs
quick in French, shoplifters at Christmastime, eighth-grade
graduates with surgically altered fingerprints, thank you
for all the Santa Claus. Now my dad's with you,
and I'm in the V.F.W. meeting room behind the bar,
as he requested, a simple service.
                                      What must you
think of me, holding forth behind my father's ashes,
every character a witness, every anecdote epic?
Do you shift your wings in heavenly chairs
if I hit a sour note? Mock boo-hoos when I speak
of the man that you knew better? A few dabs
to the eye with a silk kerchief?
Go someone, quickly,
                   fetch Little George his ringing lyre . . .

Elegy for My Mother's Ex-Boyfriend

Let it be said
that Tim's year was divided
into two seasons: sneakers
and flip-flops. Let us
remember that Tim
would sometimes throw a football
with all the requisite grip, angle
and spiral-talk. Let us recall
that for the sake of what was left
of appearances, my mother
never once let him sleep
in her bed; he snored all over
our dog-chewed couch, and in
the mornings when I tip-toed
past him on my way
to school, his jowls
fat as a catcher's mitt, I never cracked
an empty bottle across that space
where his front teeth
rotted out. Nor did I touch
a struck match to that mole
by his lip, whiskery dot that—he
believed—made him irresistible
to all lovelorn women.
Still, let us remember
sweetness: Tim lying face down,
Mom popping the zits
that dotted his broad, sun-spotted back,
which, though obviously
gross, gets the January photo
in my personal wall calendar

of what love should be,
if such a calendar
could still exist above my kitchen table
junked up with the heretos and
therefores from my
last divorce.
      Let us not forget
how my mother would slip
into her red cocktail dress
and Tim would say,
"Your mother is beautiful,"
before getting up
to go dance with someone else.
      In fairness, let me
confess that I pedaled
my ten-speed
across the Leaf River bridge
all the way to Tim's
other woman's house
and lay with that woman's daughter
beside the moon-
cold weight
of the propane tank, dumb
with liquor, numb to
the fire ants that we spread
our blanket over until
I stopped for a second
and looked up
because I wondered if
her mother could hear us,
or if Tim might not

have stood in the kitchen,
maybe looked out
the window and saw
my white ass pumping
in the moonlight,
and whispered
to himself, "That's my boy."

Kingfish

I never saw my father throw a baseball
he was no jogger
he was working the cash register at my godfather's curb store
when in saunters this guy
in a tie-dye ski mask
pointing a pistol though not impolitely
demanding cash

> *was this after your dad smoked-out with Audrey*
> *of the feather boas bad sonnets Quaaludes*
> *from the fourplex across the hall*
> *was he "nervous"*

he didn't like pot for that very reason
instead of squeezing
the trigger on this huge .357 resting on a mount just under the counter
and blowing the robber into an eternity of Funyuns
my father leans over this large jar of pickled pigs' feet
and with one left hook
knocks the poor dude out

> *did he levitate*

who

> *your dad*

not that time but how embarrassing
it must have been for that man
trying to rob my godfather's store
lying on the cement floor on the other side
of his own gun

waiting for his and my dad's
least favorite people
the cops
before they hauled the guy off in a squad car
my father shook his cuffed hand
wished him luck
a guy whose ass you kick might end up your best friend
he always said to me
never humiliate
another man

                you thought your father was special
                demigod sorcerer
                more than any regular
                golden gloves
                candidate for
                electroshock

he laid so many bricks by the eighth grade—
which is when he dropped out—
he woke one morning to discover
he'd worn the fingerprints
off his fingers
his hands like poisonous unidentifiable butterflies

                which might explain the subsequent
                albeit brief life
                of crime
                his ability to transform into fish or sparrow
                his love of watching people
                walk in and out

                                                    of normal
                                                       houses

they were trying to sell some Rolex watches

                                        you mean Folex watches
                          and how does it feel to be the son of Moses
                                          let me guess he had
                                                    a huge

IQ 165 according to the Air Force
but he was more Odysseus
as the rag wearing singer
the world his home that couldn't quite place him
but let him hang around just for the hell of it
all the wine swindlers
picking pork from their teeth with a king's daggers
having slain the last cattle of the sun
anyone can tell you he was
inexplicably charming
especially wearing
a beggar's skin
his old friends called him Kingfish

                                    in the matter of the jewelry
                                      upon which he rowed
                                       the great johnboat
                                          of enterprise

always fight the badass first

to work that job you had to tighten the nut
you had to meet Johnny Zesso
he'd give you a Rolex
tell you to take it to every pawn shop in Jackson
and let him know if anyone said it was fake
so Dad took it around
came back and reported ten pawnshops said it was real
two said fake
then Johnny said you didn't go to all the pawn shops
and he took my father downtown
and between two tall buildings
at the end of this long alley barely wide enough to pass through
without turning sideways
alley my dad said he never knew existed
there was this small OPEN sign
on a locked door
and past that
a hallway maybe thirty yards long at the end of which sat
an old Jewish man on a stool in a beautiful white suit
with these huge eyeglasses that made
his eyes blink in slow motion
he said the watch was fake
he knew
because he made it
here's ten more now go

where did your father come into contact
with this semicircle of counterfeiters criminals bandits
architectural secrets

invisible passages
in plain view

his mother's people were from Beirut

that says it all

when I was four swinging my legs
from the counter of the curb store where my godfather let me sit
elbow deep in a wide-mouth jar
of these oatmeal cookies big as classroom wall clocks
my dad picked me up
and as I was bootless in my cowboy pajamas
he carried me out
to this green Cadillac
where stood my godfather
along with Uncle R they popped the trunk
and what might have been an electric guitar
inside red velvet was in fact
a Fyodorov-Ivanov Model 1924 twin barrel
tank mount (optional) machine gun
fresh from the USSR

USS argh
what are you now
apologist for la petite mob
fleet greyhounds of your memory
matched only
by the over-groomed and useless
poodles of Lethe

I never
saw Uncle R
after that
but when my father died he called
no idea how he found my number but not for a life-
time's supply of Brylcreem
would that sweet old tater eater
have given me
his address

how bad did it get

my daughter had a fresh dirty diaper
Dad out-ran the hurricane moved in to my spare room
but his cancer returned
it was new years day 2007 and Dad wanted the bank
to give him all his money back
he's moving to the country to live with some kids
unlike me they're great
I ask if he's met them "no" he says
I ask if they even exist "no"
this is my cue that he's off his meds trending psychotic
and that whatever he says
should not upset me
he says so many things
all of which upset me soon I'm screaming *you've been nothing*
but a drain since I was six
regretting it even as I said it
he did not raise his hand
he smiled what you might call the "you're my only son" smile
as if proud of me

for veering
from a lifelong
habit of lies

what have you learned from this

never go outside without a shirt unless you're boxing or at a swimming
    pool
don't spit on concrete
you might drink Old Milwaukee or whiskey straight up
the stranger is my guest
the janitor my wisdom
treat every wandering singer in a puke-stained foreigner's drug-rug
like the Angel Gabriel

what have you learned

even when he was bat-shit crazy we both liked to err
on the side of sarcasm
but I loved him

can you pay the fine
if you can't pay the fine you'll have to stay here forever
and you're not even dead yet

I will pay the fine and exit your fine land
it really is marvelous
now will you grant him passage
it was all my fault
and we'd already
gained a new take on life together

I was clocked at 102 miles per hour
when the state trooper sped toward us like a giant pissed off magnet
on the way to Gainesville for Dad's seventh
round of chemo
I explained to the officer
his urgent need
Dad played it up rocked back and forth groaned with pain
blew phlegm through his
voice prosthesis throat-hole but the cop kept writing the ticket long as the
    state of Florida
so finally Dad raised his arm poked out his pointer finger
and moved it in tiny circles
while his other hand
fell across his eyes
Dad dubbed this move "The Dance of Lady Justice"
which I then repeated to the cop so that he could actually understand it
and the cop he couldn't get enough
he was clutching his stomach
laughing so hard the eagle insignia from his lapel
flew off toward the west
smirking its eagle head off
clutching a goose
in its talons
plucked from the household gods

3

Love Letter to You, Dear Reader

> *They sparkle still the right Promethean fire.*
> —Shakespeare, *Love's Labour's Lost*

Once, I loved a tanning-bed junkie: she'd slip
away from her midday desk, strip down
and pocket herself between oblong bulbs,
ultraviolet husk of Vitamin D, effortless
endorphin rush, which left an odd tan line
along the inner rims of her ass cheeks,
and occasionally led to the appearance
of frighteningly asymmetrical moles, none
of which especially turned me on. Still, I suppose
the daily ache—that surge of discontent
that left her convinced her untanned state
would never be enough—yes, dear
reader, that lack of self-love and spiraling
vulnerability spoke to me, drew me more
urgently toward her, she who was quite
good enough, at least for me, at least for those
few weeks when I gave up cigarettes
while she, for her part, turned pleasantly,
miraculously pale. For a while, it seemed
—lying abreast in the post-coital nest of single-
parent love—that we might rise and stroll
into a cancer-free and nearly Baptist sunset
with a happiness neither of us expected,
nor, in truth, felt we deserved. Hence,
my address to you, not her, dear silent
and literary other whose eyes I pray to move.
Do we all feel better now? Could this be
the moment when we agree to let sail
whatever we harbor of the long ago and loved?
The fact is, she's unsafely re-ensconced
in the routine of a successful and mildly

self-loathing real estate agent
among the many available George Hamilton
lookalikes that populate the professional set
of cocktail hour in Perdido Key. I read
my books, teach my classes, and keep
a lozenge squirreled away in the slack fat
of my jowl for those hours between
the appearance of friends, or a friendly
stranger, from whom I might bum the next
deadly, next gum-tingling and
delicious breath. And you? Tell the truth.
Isn't there one thing that you still
hate about yourself, that makes you more
my confidante than not, my comrade,
my dark horse, my long-shot candidate for love?

Elegy for the Epic

Returns Odysseus to a kingdom of no shank.
        No swineherd among the timber. No timber.

No scrawny Argos with tick-riddled ear.
        This epic so anti-climactic could pioneer

a fresh wave of disappearance. Now,
        shrimp boats dot the horizon like toys

in a child god's blow-up pool, the gulf
        a mono-gesture, lemon juice semi-haze.

I sit on an ice chest and fish all day.
        My surplus minnows, dull in their bucket,

spark war between the shorebirds. Still, I
        fear no castigation, no mortal wastefulness.

For every age shoulders the rebuke of its own
        karaoke love song. If I could, I'd step out

of my body and walk in five directions.
        Palm trees my map, clouds my photo album.

The last time I stood here my father
        was alive, baiting my new wife's hook.

O Anna Lynn, You Must Have Known

So truly uninformed I was when it came
to the mechanics of love, that I donned
the condom a little early; it kept falling off
on the three-mile walk before I tapped
on the glass and you shimmied out your window
and we made for the weedy hilltop where
we gazed for a nearly unbearable moment
at the moon's twin in the drainage pond
and you spread the slightly mildewed blanket
of our long-awaited consummation
while I tugged the ribbed but not quite lubricated
master of awkward ceremonies back on.
How soon you said *Is that all?* Miracle was,
there was even that much. I was so hot
for you, slobbering all over that wisp of hair
loose from the braid behind your ear,
everything sliding together just right
in the big bang universe of our love,
which must have lasted at least thirty seconds.
You sighed, tugged your jeans back on,
while I fumbled through my backpack
for to share with you—food of the gods—
a paper-clipped bag of Fritos. I remember
watching you re-snap your bra, thinking
boobs, tits, breasts, jugs, what stupid,
insufficient words. Naturally, you took up
with an older boy, though still kind
to me when we passed between classes: I held
my books in front of my crotch
trying to hide the erection that visited me,
for no apparent reason, each morning

at nine a.m. And then? Soon after we
abandoned those halls with their lockers like rows
of uniform sarcophagi, you fled
to college. Probably you married. Maybe divorced.
Maybe nothing turned out like you hoped
and you sit up smoking Pall Malls
in your nightgown, while in your kitchen window
the same moon that once graced our bodies
now illuminates nothing so much
as the most recent in a long line
of disappointments that you've grown to accept
as the ubiquitous background of your
early middle age, which has nothing
to do with me, though I still wonder
what I might say if I saw you again,
aglow beneath the nimbus of my complete
embarrassment. O Anna Lynn, sorry
to have delivered unto you my mid-pubescent
and self-maligning heart there by the pond
that we called the lagoon. But tell me
you're alone. Tell me the history of your discontent.
Tell me why you returned to me
when I sat this morning on the back porch,
waiting for the coffee, recounting
it all, the grass still wet with last night's fog.

Afterlife

Six-year-old Jody pedals in on his yellow Huffy, playing card clothespinned between the spokes because the engine sound he makes sputtering air over his lips is sweet, but not enough.

Swizzle stick in hand, my mother conducts the orchestra inside her gin and tonic, my father wheeling past in his heavenly convertible, his friend they call the "King of Sweden" in tow.

The hell of it is wanting to stay. Cuban cigars, discount Winnebagos, washtub hooch, all the people you loved closer to you than fog in a cow's mouth.

Everyone's come so far.

Hundreds of sparrows, an army of twigs, the toothy smile of a carousel stallion on an afternoon the color of birthday cake. October of sawdust and Nixon mask, star charts, war balloons, all the grown-ups getting loud in the living room, still reeling from the rides and sausage and beer, carrying on about what fell from whose pockets on the Loop-The-Loop, whose wig went crooked on the Tilt-A-Whirl.

Chicken Brick'n

Because there's no end to cruelty,
                Lyle ties half a brick
                                to a hen's foot, climbs

the ladder up the water tower
                where waits Tony—together,
                                they toss their weighted hens

into space: the flung chicken
                that charts its course
                                across clear air, fans its wings

and flaps a few feet
                with all the glory of a crippled
                                helicopter, thereby traversing

the greater distance before
                its feathers flip skyward
                                and the dud parachute

of its body descends to the weeds
                with a certain thump,
                                that chicken will be crowned

—posthumously, of course—
                Chicken Brick'n Champ.
                                In some cases, boredom

might be life at its best,
                all the suffering fixed
                                in the doomed body of one noble,

if small-brained, bird.
        I see the three of us walking
                in high grass. Lyle calls

Tony a loser. Tony predicts victory.
        We run toward feathers,
                ready for the measure, t-shirts

pulled over our heads
        in the hooded manner
                of the great Pharaohs.

Gods of wingéd dignity,
        have mercy. We take our
                positions. We count our steps.

There's Nothing Wrong with You

Dear twelve-year-old boy who eats frozen waffles three times a day while your mother makes a run for gas station chicken with every meth-shooting hard-leg in Pascagoula,

yea though I sit here choking down a po-boy with the crickets in my wisdom, triumphant and twice divorced, I wish I could write a happier poem for you.

If the water gets turned off, you can still drink from the bug-peppered oasis of your neighbor's plastic swimming pool.

I wish it would stop raining long enough for me to throw a football with such a perfect spiral that my twelve-year-old self could catch it.

I found *Classics of Western Thought, Vol 1.* and *Complete Tabla-ture: Paul Simon's Greatest Hits* in the dumpster behind my grand-father's.

That June, I took up residence in Plato's cave and all the above-ground graves and hostile Boudreauxs and Heberts of Chackbay, Louisiana, became a sweltering yet tolerable allegory.

I hope you never shoot up half the day just to shoot up half the day.

I hope you never compare the frozen waffles of youth to the frozen waffles of prison.

I sawed off a two-by-four, then drew six vertical strings with a black magic marker, fifteen short lines crosswise for frets and hummed the melody to "Me and Julio," strumming that rotten ass rain-warped board.

It's not always right to blame your mother.

There must be fifty ways to leave a mess.

Fifty ways to kick a skanky habit over and over.

Fifty ways to cook waffles when you're twelve, when the day outlasts the soap operas and it's impossibly hot in the parking lot of the apartment complex where no other kids seem to live,

when the nights are streetlights, mean and skinny, and the morning belongs to no one except the quiet, and time, and hunger, for which you are entirely suited.

Ever read *The Book of There's Nothing Wrong with You?*

Me neither.

Nonetheless, they punched my free-lunch card.

Nor is it right to hate God, or anyone else busy sleeping in the blue casket of summer, bold with constellations.

The Guitar Boat

You know after death, you have to go by yourself.
—Blind Willie Johnson

When I brush the strings with my sleeves, pulling the oars back,
I hear the lagoon music of a blues dream in which I ferry
my father's ashes, though the song I sing is no funeral song,
      and I carry his ashes only
            when the oars part the air
                  inside this dream I have of Venice,
                        asleep in Mississippi.

When I brush the strings with my sleeves, I carry my father
to meet my father, that he might hear the music the way
that ships, clouds, mirrors hear the music. When I brush
      the strings with my sleeves, it is
            my father returning to this dream
                  in which I ferry toward him, and away,
                      singing, laughing, always

disappearing, always music. When I cry, I cry backward
in the direction of my rowing, tears like crystal minnows
leaping back into my eyes. I know, I know, rowing his ashes,
      clouds move in the mirror when
            the mirror moves. I will meet you
                back home, ferry you
                    across the long water. There is

no balm like the blue sleep of water. This music, my father,
tears like crystal minnows swimming off ahead of me,
salt smell of the lagoon. Goodbye strings, goodbye song,
      guitar that is a ferry
            for the child of ashes,
                music of street vendors
                  from the widening shore.

Not Soul

as greater than the sum
of what's missing. We
all want our people back.
Not soul as bicycle
in the body's hurricane.
Nor soul held hostage
in the cat-haunted alley
of my skull where anyone
can hear the wind
between pigeons.
Not soul as groom
to the bride of everything,
soul scribbled on
the highest leaf
of the tree in flames,
theory of soul etched
on a bee's wing. Not soul
as the whole-
note hum of zero. Nothing
that personal.
Nor the sound they
made walking through
the house, first
communion, prefix
of distance, infinity
seen through a tire-
swing lens, total of all
prescriptions. I mean
the soul as sleep
when the best we
can do is dream

of them, who once lived
here, now clear
filament. Soul spun
from the vanishing.

Heuristic for the Nearsighted

For years I felt below snuff, stacked
        one improbable sky atop another,
                carried nails in a fish net, forced
                        myself to use a rotary phone for the routine

payment of bills. Campaign with no
        election, or rather a daily election
                in which said candidate replaces
                        his platform with a mirror because

people can *see* in mirrors, especially when
        there's several mirrors, or better,
                one mirror, the very last authentic
                        mirror, starlets tossing their shades

for a watery glimpse. Where was I?
        Yes—the necessity of error. Two
                eyes are definitely better. Third eye
                        for cosmic measure. But four's a crowd, I thought.

To hell with four! On the other hand, taking notes
        in Old Testament Greek is difficult
                without them. Correction: Four
                        is Four-ever! Everybody likes old four-eyes.

Who once was verboten, now's cool.
        Better to be insufficient, than forgotten.
        In this way, we move forward.
                Down on all fours, sweet Lord, for you.

Michelle McFatter

JAMES KIMBRELL was born in Jackson, Mississippi. He has published two previous volumes of poetry, *The Gatehouse Heaven* and *My Psychic*, and was co-translator of *Three Poets of Modern Korea: Yi Sang, Hahm Dong-Seon, and Choi Young-Mi*. His work has appeared in magazines such as *Poetry, The Cincinnati Review, Ploughshares, Field, The New Guard*, and *Best American Poetry 2012*. He has been the recipient of the Discovery / *The Nation* Award, a Whiting Writers' Award, the Ruth Lilly Fellowship, the Bess Hokin Prize from *Poetry* magazine, and a fellowship from the National Endowment for the Arts. He currently resides in Tallahassee where he teaches in the creative writing program at Florida State University.

Sarabande Books is a nonprofit literary press located in Louisville, KY and Brooklyn, NY. Founded in 1994 to champion poetry, short fiction, and essay, we are committed to creating lasting editions that honor exceptional writing. For more information, please visit sarabandebooks.org.